HEALING
POWER
for the
HEART

Robert Abel

Valentine Publishing House
Denver, Colorado

Valentine Publishing House LLC
P.O. Box 27422
Denver, Colorado 80227

The Scripture quotations contained herein are from the New Revised Standard Version Bible, copyright 1989, Division of Christian Education of the National Council of the Churches of Christ in the United States of America. Used by permission. All rights reserved.

Cover Graphics—Desert Isle Design LLC

Library of Congress Control Number: 2006926964

Publisher's Cataloging-in-Publication Data

Abel, Robert.
    Healing Power for the Heart / Robert Abel / 2nd Edition.

       p. : ill. ; cm.

    ISBN–10: 0-9711536-9-8
    ISBN–13: 978-0-9711536-9-1
    Includes bibliographical references.

1. Spiritual healing. 2. Healing—Religious aspects—Christianity. 3. Emotions—Religious aspects—Christianity. 4. Love—Religious aspects—Christianity. I. Title.

BT732.5 .A245 2006
234/.131

                        2006926964

Printed in the United States of America.

Table of Contents

I pray that, according to the riches of his glory,
he may grant that you may be strengthened
in your inner being with power through his Spirit,
and that Christ may dwell in your hearts through faith,
as you are being rooted and grounded in love.

Ephesians 3:16–17

Introduction

Resting in the shade of a palm tree near the old stone well, Jesus noticed a woman approaching from a distance. She was carrying a clay vessel in one hand and a rope in the other. "Please give me a drink of water," he said as she drew closer.

The voice coming from beneath the tree startled the woman. After stopping to see who was speaking to her, she said in a defensive tone, *"How is it that you, a Jew, ask a drink of me, a woman of Samaria?"*[1]

Jesus stood up, reached out his hand and said, *"If you knew the gift of God, and who it is that is saying to you, 'Give me a drink,' you would have asked him, and he would have given you living water."*[2]

As the power of the Holy Spirit began to minister to the woman, her heart softened. *"Sir, you have no bucket, and the well is deep. Where do you get that living water?"*[3]

"Everyone who drinks of this water will be thirsty again, but those who drink of the water that I will give them will never be thirsty. The water that I will give will become in them a spring of water gushing up to eternal life."[4]

As the Lord's words pierced her heart, she remembered the stories about a prophet long ago who spoke of living water flowing from the temple. It started out as a small stream and eventually turned into a mighty river. Wherever the living water flowed, it brought new life to the dry and thirsty land.

As the woman gazed into the Lord's eyes, she could feel his tender compassion. Just being in his presence made her feel safe enough to ask, *"Sir, give me this water, so that I may never be thirsty or have to keep coming here to draw water."*[5]

"Go, call your husband, and come back."[6]

Immediately she looked away and said, *"I have no husband."*[7]

"You are right in saying, 'I have no husband'; for you have had five husbands, and the one you have now is not your husband."[8]

After the truth was disclosed, the woman was able to step into the light of the Lord's presence. She felt ashamed for trying to hide her past. She was sick of living in the darkness. She had spent her whole life looking for love in all the wrong places. Many men from her past had hurt her, others took advantage of her, still others criticized everything she did.

All Jesus wanted to do was fill her empty vessel with his divine love. He wanted to heal all her wounds, but before he could do so, she needed to embrace the painful events from her past and acknowledge the truth by saying, *"What you have said is true!"*[9]

After she opened her heart and embraced the pain

from her past, the Lord's life-giving water flowed into her dry and empty soul. She was so excited she *left her water jar and went back to the city. She said to the people, "Come and see a man who told me everything I have ever done!"*[10]

In the same way, Jesus wants a mighty river of his life-giving water flowing from all the living temples of all his beloved sons and daughters. He wants to create a divine partnership with you. The Lord came so that you *may have life, and have it abundantly.*[11]

He is calling you right now. *"Let anyone who is thirsty come to me, and let the one who believes in me drink. As the scripture has said, 'Out of the believer's heart shall flow rivers of living water.'"*[12]

What are you waiting for? Jesus has incredible plans for your life. He wants to establish a passionate love affair with you. He wants to give you life to the fullest. He wants to heal all your traumatic past experiences, so that you can experience the fullness of his extravagant love.

1
Offer an Invitation to Jesus

Many years ago the Lord showed me a vision of my heart. I was sitting on the floor praying when the power of the Holy Spirit overshadowed me. I could feel the supernatural grandeur and majesty of God all around.

When the Lord showed me my heart, it was small, cold and insignificant. It looked like it was made out of metal and had a tiny door that opened and closed. In that moment of truth, I realized that I had never invited the divine presence of God to dwell inside of my heart.

God's grandeur was bright and brilliant like a vast ocean of pure love, truth and warmth. It was too much for me to endure. After a brief moment, the vision grew too intense, and I had to break away. A few moments later, I found myself back in my bedroom sitting on the floor.

I took the calling from God very seriously. I got back in prayer and recreated the vision from my memory. I pictured the metal heart and imagined a tiny door opening as I prayed the words, *I invite you into my heart, Jesus. Please come and dwell inside of me.*

Nothing happened, so I tried opening the door wider and praying harder, but nothing changed. I didn't feel any different. I knew the vision was from God and that it was true. I was withholding my heart because I was scared. Deep down inside of me I was reluctant to give God the most sacred part of my being.

Who knows what God would do to me if I gave him my everything. He could give me the most difficult of all missionary assignments, and if he had full control of my life, he could cause me all kinds of torment until I completed whatever he had asked.

After thinking about the vision, I realized I was scared to give my heart to God, because I have been hurt many times in the past. Whenever I gave my heart to a beautiful woman, it usually turned out disastrous. I have fallen in love several times, and after I opened up my heart to these women, they had the ability to cause me a lot of pain.

Falling in love is the richest and most passionate experience I have ever encountered, but unfortunately the breakups can be devastating. Not only did my girlfriends have the ability to hurt me after I had fallen in love with them, but they could also take advantage of my vulnerability.

After thinking about this further, I realized I was projecting my human-relationship dynamics upon the Deity. I was scared to invite Jesus into the most sacred parts of my being, because every time I had invited a woman into my heart, I ended up getting hurt.

After thinking about the vast beauty and magnificence of God's grandeur in comparison to my emptiness, I was forced to make a decision. I could live my life with a cold heart, or I could invite the richness, beauty and splendor of the Lord to dwell inside of me.

Eventually, I made a decision for Christ. I centered myself in deep prayer and recalled the vision of the tiny heart. I spoke the words from the core of my being: *"Dear Jesus, I confess you as my Lord and Savior. Please do anything you want with my life. I surrender everything into your hands. Come into my heart and create in me the kind of person you have intended me to be."*

After my prayer time, I didn't feel any different. The vast ocean of God's great love didn't fill me to overflowing, and soon I began to worry. I called a spiritual friend to pray with me. She invited me over to her house, and after I shared the vision with her, we decided to go to the mountains and pray some more.

We drove about 30 minutes, and after parking the car, we walked up a dirt road toward the top of the mountain. The sun was about to set for the evening, and the sky was illuminated in a thousand different shades of yellow and orange.

After we arrived at the top, we sat on a rock outcrop and watched the sparkling city lights below. With the unspoken words of my inner being I invited Jesus to come inside. In the same way a man falls in love with a woman, I opened up my heart and fell in love with Jesus. I surrendered the core of my being to him.

I made myself vulnerable to him in every way, as I gave him my everything.

Immediately, I could feel his euphoric strength enter into me. It was just like Jesus had promised when he said, *"Those who love me will keep my word, and my Father will love them, and we will come to them and make our home with them."*[1]

The divine presences of Christ had finally filled my heart, and the next day, I was on a spiritual high. I could actually feel the presence of Jesus inside of me. Whenever I started to pray, a great wellspring of living water would rise up inside of me.

Before my encounter with Jesus, it would take me several hours of prayer to reach the deep levels that I now experience after just a few short minutes. Before the mountaintop experience, it felt like God was somewhere up in the clouds, distant and far away. When I prayed, it felt like my prayers to God would hit the top of my head and stop.

Now when I pray, Jesus is right here inside of me. His presence dwells inside of my soul. I don't need to shoot prayer arrows into the clouds anymore. I can commune with the Lord anytime I want. I have the testimony of the Son of God living inside of me just as it's described in Sacred Scripture: *Those who believe in the Son of God have the testimony in their hearts. Whoever has the Son has life; whoever does not have the Son of God does not have life.*[2]

After my mountaintop experience, even the words *I love you, Jesus,* took on a whole new meaning. Before they didn't mean much, because I had never met

Jesus. I had read about Jesus in the Bible and heard many people talking about him in church. I knew who he was, but I never had a real live encounter with the risen Lord until the day I invited him into my heart. After meeting Jesus, I could feel my love for the Lord welling up inside of me every time I said the words, *I love you, Jesus.*

After my conversion experience, my ministry efforts excelled greatly. I had been attending daily Mass for the last 10 years, and I was serving the Lord in full-time ministry, but I never felt very comfortable talking to people about Jesus.

A part of me didn't want to force my beliefs on others, but after the God of the universe started dwelling inside of me, I immediately acquired a burning desire to share the richness of Jesus with everybody I knew. If my friends didn't have the Spirit of Christ dwelling inside of their hearts, they were missing out on the greatest blessing of all.

Have you ever invited the divine presence of Jesus to dwell inside of your heart? Was there ever a time when you opened up your soul in complete surrender to the Lord? Have you ever fallen deeply in love with Jesus and invited his Spirit to dwell inside of you?

You may want to take some time right now to pray. Find a quiet place in your home, at church or on a mountaintop. Dig down deep into your heart and offer the Lord's Spirit an invitation to come inside of your soul. Fall in love with Jesus the same way you would fall in love with a romantic lover.

The God of the universe deeply desires to create a

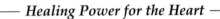

passionate love affair with you. Plunge deep into the vast ocean of his divine love and allow the sacred romance to begin.

2
Acknowledge the Painful Truth

A soft glow from the full moon provided enough light for the Lord and his disciples to ascend the Mount of Olives. Upon entering the garden, Jesus turned to his companions and said, *"You will all become deserters because of me this night; for it is written, 'I will strike the shepherd, and the sheep of the flock will be scattered.'"*[1]

Peter stepped forward and said, *"Though all become deserters because of you, I will never desert you."*[2]

"Truly I tell you, this very night, before the cock crows, you will deny me three times."[3]

"Even though I must die with you, I will not deny you,"[4] Peter said.

Soon afterward an angry mob armed with swords and clubs appeared. The guards who were with them grabbed Jesus and forced him to the ground. Fear seized all the disciples, and after a brief struggle, they all fled into the night.

The guards fastened heavy chains with shackles

around the Lord's hands and feet. They started screaming at him to move forward, pushing him to move faster. Eventually they reached the high priest's house and entered the courtyard.

Some of the men from the group started placing firewood in a circular pit. After a fire had been started, Peter cautiously approached from the distance. He joined the men who were standing around the fire to see what would happen next.

As he was warming his hands near the glow of the firelight, a servant girl recognized him and said, *"This man also was with him."*[5] Everybody turned to look at Peter. Several soldiers drew their swords. Peter stepped forward and spoke in a soft voice, *"Woman, I do not know him."*[6]

He was able to convince the soldiers, but a little while later someone else said to him, *"You also are one of them."* But Peter said, *"Man, I am not!"*[7]

Meanwhile, the chief priests continued questioning Jesus. A large crowd had gathered and many people started accusing Jesus of blasphemy. Others were outraged because he claimed to be God's Son. After listening to all the accusations, one man turned toward Peter and said, *"Surely this man also was with him; for he is a Galilean."*[8]

"Man, I do not know what you are talking about!"[9] Peter said.

At that moment a cock crowed, and the Lord turned to look at him. Peter had to turn away when he remembered the Lord's words, *"Before the cock crows today, you will deny me three times."*[10]

Peter loved Jesus, yet he was scared to death because of the violent crowd. Fear had crept into his heart, and now his relationship with the Lord was damaged. When Jesus needed him the most, Peter denied his very existence.

Afterward, Peter *went out and wept bitterly.*[11] He lay face-down in an open field, wondering how he could ever look into the Lord's eyes again. The internal anguish he was experiencing was unbearable. All Peter could do was suffer. After spending several hours in agony, he eventually distanced himself from his emotions to escape the torment of his heart.

Over the next few days, Peter began growing colder and even more distant. He wanted to withdraw from the memories because every time someone mentioned how the soldiers had driven a crown of thorns into the Lord's head, it made him sick. Stories of the crucifixion brought up even more pain, which he was trying so desperately to avoid.

It grew so bad that within a short period of time, Peter wanted to go back to his old way of life. He said to the sons of Zebedee, *"I am going fishing."*[12]

"We will go with you,"[13] they said.

After the men gathered some supplies, they put out to sea. They worked hard all night but caught nothing. Just after daybreak, Jesus stood on the shore and called out to them, *"Cast the net to the right side of the boat, and you will find some."*[14]

The men didn't know what to think, but they cast

the net into the sea one more time. As they began to pull the four corners together, the water started tingling with life. There were so many fish, it was impossible to draw the net into the boat.

That disciple whom Jesus loved said to Peter, "It is the Lord!"[15]

Immediately, all the events from the past started flashing before Peter's eyes. The only thing that would make Peter feel better would be reconciliation with the Lord. He wanted to apologize and make things right, but he felt so unworthy. All Peter could do was put on some clothes and jump into the water.

The other disciples came to the shore dragging the net full of fish behind them. When they saw the charcoal fire, they approached with great apprehension. Jesus said to them, *"Bring some of the fish that you have just caught."*[16]

After they finished eating the meal, Jesus said to Peter, *"Simon son of John, do you love me more than these?"*[17]

"Yes, Lord; you know that I love you."[18]

A second time Jesus said to him, *"Simon son of John, do you love me?"*[19]

"Yes, Lord; you know that I love you."[20]

The Lord asked the third time, *"Simon son of John, do you love me?"*[21]

Peter felt hurt because he said to him the third time, "Do you love me?" And he said to him, "Lord, you know everything; you know that I love you."[22]

Jesus said to him, *"Feed my sheep."*[23]

Before Peter could be reconciled to the Lord, he had to go back into his past and work through all the negative events that were separating him from the Lord's love. Peter needed to address his guilty feelings and allow the Lord to wash him clean.

Once Peter acknowledged his mistakes, the light and love of Christ entered his heart, and he was set free. Jesus accepted him back into his intimate fellowship and restored his position in the ministry as the leader of the newly established church.

In the same way, if you desire a deeper and more passionate relationship with Jesus, spend some time right now in prayer. Ask the Lord to show you if there are any hurtful events from your past that are preventing the fullness of his love from residing deep within your soul.

After you examine your heart, ask the Holy Spirit to start the process of reconciliation. There's nothing to fear. Jesus loves you. He has incredible plans for your life. Accept his merciful love right now, and allow his tender compassion to wash you clean.

3

Wash in His
Life-Giving Water

One day I received a letter from a young lady named Susan. Her mom had died of cancer when she was a little girl, and to make matters worse, all during her childhood her father was abusive toward her and neglectful.

As I read her letter, I was filled with compassion for her situation. I could feel the Lord's love welling up in my heart for his precious daughter, as she wrote the following request for help:

I'm an overeater and I'm starting to break down. I just feel this mental block when I ask Jesus for help. I used to be really religious and attended church on a regular basis.

I have never felt like I was good enough and still feel like I'm going to hell. I feel so bound up. How can I get Jesus to come into my life again? Why would he want to? I feel so unworthy and unloved. I live with my boyfriend, and I feel terrible and shameful.

After reading Susan's letter, I began praying for the

Lord's guidance. I knew Jesus had a burning desire to set his precious daughter free. He wanted to heal all her wounds and establish his kingdom deep within her soul.

Jesus had all the healing power and grace that Susan needed to break free from the bondage that was holding her back. The only question was, what was keeping Susan from accepting the Lord's love? When I asked Susan about this, she responded by saying:

I have watched many people in my church talk about their relationship with the Lord while they continued to engage in premarital sex. I don't know how they do it, because I feel so guilty and ashamed. I feel like a dirty rag that should be thrown away.

What's very clear to me right now is that having sex is what led me away from God. Because of my abusive relationship with my father, I searched for love in the arms of men. I have settled for the wrong people and have gotten involved in relationships that are not healthy.

There were a few one-night stands, and these really hurt. They made me feel used and abandoned.

I guess what's keeping me away from God is that I am afraid, guilty and ashamed. I feel like such a let-down to God and his Word. Most of all I feel like a let-down to myself. After I compromised my integrity, I became ashamed and turned away from God.

After reading Susan's letter, I could feel the Lord's desire to wash his precious daughter clean. It was the same kind of love the Lord used to wash the disciples clean. Jesus has so much love that during the night of his betrayal, he stood up, took off his outer robe, and tied a towel around his waist. *Then he poured water into a basin and began to wash the disciples' feet and to wipe them with the towel that was tied around him.*[1]

When the Lord approached Peter, he objected by saying, *"Lord, are you going to wash my feet?"*[2]

"You do not know now what I am doing, but later you will understand,"[3] Jesus said.

"You will never wash my feet,"[4] Peter said.

"Unless I wash you, you have no share with me."[5]

The Lord had so much love that he assumed the role of the lowest servant and washed the disciples' feet after they had been walking around on the dirty roads of Jerusalem all day. In the same way that the Lord washed the disciples clean, he also wanted to wash Susan clean. After spending more time in prayer, I responded to Susan's request for help by sending her the following exercise:

Please spend some time in prayer and picture yourself in the Gospel scene next to Peter. Try to imagine what the upper room looked like. Look into Peter's eyes and try to identify with whatever forms of pride that were preventing him from allowing the Lord to wash him clean.

After you can identify with Peter, look into the Lord's eyes. Listen to him as he speaks the same words to you, *"Unless I wash you, you have no share with me."*

After you have finished mediating on the Gospel message, I would like to ask you to allow Jesus to wash you clean. Please go to your bathtub and invite Jesus to wash your feet. I realize that Jesus will not show up in person to wash your feet, so you are going to have to do the washing part yourself; but I believe that Jesus will be there in Spirit.

I want you to put your heart into this assignment. I want you to tenderly wash your feet and allow Jesus to minister to your spirit as you are doing so.

A few days later, Susan responded to the exercise by saying:

At first I didn't want to do your assignment, but after reading the scripture passage, I realized my objections were coming from pride with a great sense of awe.

Jesus is perfect, and I am not. I feel so unworthy having the perfect Savior washing my dirty feet.

I will admit to you that it was very hard for me at first, but after I started it felt much easier. As I was scrubbing, it felt like I was washing off years of hurt and pain from walking the wrong paths in life. The thought of it made me cry. I truly felt Jesus was there with me, and I know he is here with me now.

I want you to know that I'm going to church today for the first time in five years. I hope to reach out to God and let him know how sorry I am for everything and let him know how much he means to me.

After reading Susan's letter, I started to cry. The Lord showed up in a profound way and ministered to his precious daughter. Once Susan was able to reestablish her relationship with God, her life started turning around. She was able to make the right decisions concerning her relationships, and soon afterward God began the process of healing all her emotional wounds.

In the same way, if you would like to experience a deeper encounter with the Lord's love, take some time and allow Jesus to wash you clean. Start by meditating on the Scripture passage from John 13. Place yourself next to Peter, and after you accept the Lord's love, invite the Spirit of Jesus to join you as wash away all the pain and mistakes from your past.

For as the heavens are high above the earth, so great is his steadfast love toward those who fear him; as far as the east is from the west, so far he removes our transgressions from us.[6]

Jesus wants to make himself very real to you. Take some time right now to accept his merciful love. After you have washed in his life-giving waters, ask the Lord if there are any events from your past that he wants you to write about.

4

Write Some
Healing Letters

When the Lord formed me inside of my mother's womb, he gave me his own heart, character and divine nature. According to Genesis 1:26, I was created in the image and likeness of God, and I didn't come into this world with any kind of critical, angry, abusive or fear-driven tendencies.

As I was growing up, the divine nature that God had given me slowly started to change. Every time I was hurt as a little boy, I would seek my parents' love and support. If I received their love, my hurt would be healed, and I would feel better.

Whenever I was hurt and didn't receive the love and support that I needed, I would suffer for a short period of time and then repress that hurt deep within my soul. Over time, all the unresolved hurt that I had repressed slowly affected my God-given natural programming. My pure and innocent nature slowly disappeared, and a negative and critical spirit took its place.

I didn't even know I was critical until some of my girlfriends started pointing it out to me. I would treat them the same way my father treated my mother. I didn't know any better. When one of my girlfriends did something that didn't meet my expectations, I would speak critical words to her and hurt her in the same way that I had been hurt.

After going through several painful breakups, I decided to work on my negative attitude. At first I tried to eliminate the unhealthy tendencies using cognitive therapy. I tried thinking less-critical thoughts. I tried to stop myself from speaking critical words whenever someone did something to me that I didn't like.

The cognitive approach didn't work, because every time I tried stopping myself from making negative remarks, I could feel a raging monster welling up inside of me. The more I prayed for deliverance, the more God started bringing up all my repressed anger toward my father.

On a conscious level, I wasn't angry at my father. I love my dad. He's a good man. I grew up just like him. We get along great. On the surface I wasn't mad at my father, but deep inside my heart, I had a ton of repressed hurt.

I started the process of forgiving my father by writing a healing letter. After setting aside some time for prayer, I began writing a letter to my father, expressing all my repressed feelings. I wanted to get it all out, so that I could invite more of the Lord's loving presence to dwell inside of my heart.

Before I started writing the letter, I pictured my father in a completely healed state standing before Jesus. After looking into his eyes and after feeling the

Lord's love in my heart, I wrote my father the following letter:

Dear Dad,

I'm writing you this letter to express my feelings. You were very negative and critical all during my childhood. You never had anything nice to say to me, and it hurts! Why didn't you ever tell me how much you cared? All I wanted was your love and approval. I looked up to you. You were my everything. I'm angry. I didn't deserve to be treated like that! I'm sad, because I wanted a more loving father. I'm sad because I wanted your love and approval, and it feels like I never received it.

I wish we could go back and change the past. I'm sorry I didn't meet your expectations. I'm sorry we didn't have a closer relationship. I'm sorry for any wrong that I have caused you. I know you didn't mean to hurt me. I know you were a sweet innocent little boy (just like me) who was hurt by your father. I'm sorry that you suffered the same way I did. Let's rebuild our relationship and start all over. I love you.

Signed your son, Rob

After writing the first letter to my father, I wanted to hear him apologize. After venting all my hurt on paper, I wanted to replace the negativity with the Lord's love. It wouldn't do any good to go around life venting negativity everywhere. In order to complete the healing process, I needed to invite the Lord's love into my wounded heart.

To finish the letter-writing exercise, I pictured my father standing next to Jesus. I asked the Lord to speak the loving words on my father's behalf that I needed to hear. If my father was in a completely healed state, full of God's love, he would have spoken the same words to me. But because we are all somewhere on the healing journey, I allowed the Lord's love to flow through my father, as I wrote the following response on his behalf:

Dear Son,

I'm so sorry. I never knew how badly I hurt you. I did the best I could. I wanted to be the best father in the world for you. I'm sorry, I tried my best. I never meant to hurt you with my negative comments. All I wanted was for you to grow up and be the best you could be. Please don't hold this against me. I'm sorry, please forgive me. I understand how you feel. I grew up with a critical father myself. I love you a lot. I'm very proud of you. You mean the world to me.

Signed, Dad

After I wrote this letter on my father's behalf, the walls that I had built around my heart started to come down. At first I couldn't believe I wrote the letter. As I read it over and over, I broke down and started crying. The words moved from my head to my heart, and I was able to accept my father's love and forgive him.

An enormous hurt that I had carried around for years was gone, and now God's love resided in its place. It was such a powerful experience, I physically felt lighter afterward. After forgiving my father, my critical nature disappeared and my God-given natural programming was restored to its original condition.

If you would like to restore your God-given natural programming back to its original condition, take some time right now and ask the Lord to show you any events from your past that are in need of his healing touch.

After the Lord brings up a memory in your prayer time, start by picturing that person in your imagination. Begin writing a healing letter that you never intend to send. Vent all the hurt that you have been carrying around for years on paper. Ask the Lord to help you dig down deep inside of your heart and get it all out. Give all of it to him. Don't hold anything back.

After you have released all the hurt and negativity on paper, picture the person who hurt you standing next to Jesus, full of God's love. Allow Jesus to speak to you on his or her behalf. Write down all the loving words that you deserve to hear.

Allow the Lord's love to flow into your heart. Release everything to the Lord. Forgive the person who hurt you. Say the words out loud, *I forgive you for hurting me.* Speak some loving words to the person who hurt you. Allow the Lord's love to flow through your heart and into the life of the person who hurt you.

Close your prayer time by discarding the letters and releasing everything to the Lord. Ask him to seal everything up with his most precious blood. By forgiving the people from your past, you will be making more room for the Spirit of Jesus to reside deep within your soul.

5

Practice the
Healing Meditation

After I discovered the profound grace in writing healing letters, I started writing them on every subject imaginable. I wrote healing letters to my parents, old girlfriends and schoolteachers. I even wrote a letter to a bee colony, because one of its members stung me when I was a little boy.

After I wrote more than a hundred healing letters, the Lord showed me an even more powerful technique. The process is similar to the letter-writing exercise, except it uses contemplative prayer and meditation to invite the Lord's healing power into the negative past experience.

I usually start the exercise with serious prayer. After I set aside a block of time to quiet my mind, I picture myself on the beach. I try to bring the scene alive in my imagination. I picture the seagulls hovering overhead and waves rolling up on the shore. I allow myself to smell the sea breeze and feel the warmth of the sun on my face.

After I'm comfortable and relaxed at the beach, I

invite Jesus to join me. I picture him sitting beside me in his white robe. I look into his eyes and talk to him. If for some reason I'm unable to look Jesus in the eyes, or fail to experience his presence with me, I keep working on the situation until I find out why my relationship with God has been hindered.

If I have unconfessed sins on my soul, I ask for his forgiveness and accept his loving embrace. Once I'm in right relationship with Jesus, I take his hand and ask him to go back in time to heal any events from my past that are still interfering with my God-given natural programming.

On one occasion the Lord brought up a memory from my childhood. The little boy from my past (I call him little Robbie) spilled a glass of milk. My mom, dad, younger brother and two sisters were all sitting around the dinner table. As soon as the glass tipped over, milk spread out in a white pool and ran through the crack in the center of the table.

As Jesus and I entered the scene, my parents were acting as if the world was about to end. I could feel anger rising up inside of me. Little Robbie hadn't meant to spill the milk. It was an accident. He felt bad enough and didn't need everybody screaming at him.

After entering the scene, I asked Jesus for the necessary grace and then began ministering to little Robbie. I lifted the little boy out of his chair and held him in my arms. "It's not your fault," I said. "I know you didn't spill the milk on purpose. Please don't feel bad. I love you. You are a good little boy regardless of how much milk gets spilled."

After little Robbie was felling better, I introduced my family to Jesus. As soon as I did, the power of the Holy Spirit started softening everybody's hearts. I could tell by looking into my parent's eyes that they knew it was wrong for them to yell at little Robbie.

When I asked them to apologize for their inappropriate actions, my mother stood up and apologized to the Lord first. Then she took little Robbie out of my arms and said to him, "I'm very sorry. Please forgive me. I shouldn't have yelled at you. It's only milk, and you are way more important to me than spilled milk will ever be."

As I watched the love of Christ soften my father's heart, I broke down and started crying. "I'm sorry too, Dad. For all these years I have been angry at you. I don't want to be angry anymore. I want to be loving like Jesus. Please forgive me for all the times I have hurt you, too."

As I went to give my father a hug, the Lord put his healing hands around both of us. After we embraced in each other's arms, I told little Robbie that I would come back and visit him as often as I could. After kissing my family good-bye, Jesus and I returned to the scene on the beach. After asking the Lord to seal everything up in his precious blood, I thanked him for giving me the necessary grace to go back and forgive my parents.

The same healing power that allowed me to go back in time is available for you right now. Jesus transcends time. He is not limited by time or space. When you give the Lord permission, he will go back in time with you to heal every situation from your past in which you have been hurt.

You can start the process right now by setting aside some time for prayer. After you quiet your mind and remove all distractions from your environment, simply invite Jesus to make himself very real to you. Picture what he looks like. Speak to him as if he were standing in front of you. Give him a hug. Look into his eyes.

After you spend a lot of time developing an authentic relationship with the Lord, ask him to go back into your past with you to a time when you were hurt. Allow the Lord's Spirit to bring to mind a hurtful event that needs his healing touch.

Once the Lord shows you something, allow your present-day self to go back and minister to the hurt little boy or girl from your childhood. If schoolchildren were being mean to you, go back and minister to the entire classroom. Tell the kids about Jesus. Introduce them to the Lord, and have them ask for his forgiveness.

If you find yourself being abused by authority figures, ask the Lord to bring along his mighty warring angels. After you confront the people who hurt you, allow the Lord's Spirit to cut through the hardness of their hearts. Picture them bowing down and asking the Lord for forgiveness.

After these people apologize for their inappropriate actions, it may be helpful to remove the hurt little boy or girl from the abusive situation. Just ask Jesus where he would like to go next. Allow the little child to take the Lord's hand and follow Jesus to a warm, safe place.

By spending the necessary time ministering to that hurt little boy or girl from your past, you will be restoring your God-given natural programming to its original condition.

6

Fall into His Loving Arms

After experiencing many deep and profound encounters with the Lord through the healing meditation, I decided to call my father to offer him the same opportunity. I started the conversation by saying, "You should give it a try. Jesus wants to take away all your pain and replace it with his extravagant love."

"How does this healing meditation work?" he asked.

"Just make a list of the ten worst things that have ever happened to you, and I will come over next week to help you work through them."

After praying for my father all week, I drove over to his house early one afternoon. Because my mother was out running errands, we had several hours of uninterrupted time to be with the Lord.

Upon entering my father's house, I took a seat on the living room floor and asked my dad to sit back in his favorite chair to relax. We started the exercise in prayer. I asked my father to close his eyes and focus on an event from his past that he wanted to heal. He began by saying, "Growing up on the farm was hard work. Times were tough back in those days...

"Well, one day we were drying potatoes on a flatbed trailer. It was a sunny day, but the sky turned cloudy, and it started to rain. Your grandfather didn't want the potatoes getting wet because we had to store them in the cellar all winter. If the potatoes were not completely dry, they would start growing sprouts.

"I wanted to help my father maneuver the trailer into the barn, so I offered to steer the front axle while he pushed from behind."

Suddenly, my father opened his eyes and looked at me as if he were about to cry. "It's okay, Dad," I said. "Jesus is going to heal you. Just close your eyes and stay with the scene."

"All I wanted to do was help get the potatoes into the barn," my dad said with a faint voice. "But I didn't steer the trailer with a wide enough radius, and the front wheel hit the barn door and stopped. By now it was raining harder than ever, so my father picked up a two-by-four and started beating me with it."

"It's okay, Dad, Jesus is going to heal you," I said. "Let's invite Jesus into the scene to help the little boy. I want you to go back with Jesus to minister to little Richard. Will you do that?"

"Yes," my father said. "I can see Jesus standing by the trailer, and I can also picture myself there too."

"Very good. Now, I want you to take the two-by-four out of your father's hand and tell him it's not right to hit the little boy."

"As soon as my father realized that Jesus had been watching him the entire time, he dropped the stick," my dad said. "I can tell by the way he is acting that he regrets his actions."

"Very good," I said. "Now, I want you to pick up the little boy and hold him in your arms. Tell him that it's not his fault."

When I looked up at my father, tears were streaming down his face. By the way he was sitting in his chair, it looked like he was holding the hurt little boy in his arms. He held little Richard a long time before I asked him if his father was ready to apologize.

"Yes," my dad said. "He's very sorry. I can picture my father kneeling down to apologize to Jesus, and then he takes little Richard from my arms and says, 'Please forgive me.' He can barely speak because he is sobbing so much. Jesus comes over and wraps his loving arms around us both."

"Very good! How does the little boy feel now?" I asked.

"He feels much better. He's happy once again," my father said.

"When you're ready, say goodbye to little Richard. Ask him if there's anything fun that he would like to do so that you can leave him in that warm, safe place with Jesus. Tell your father that you love him very much and that you will come back and visit him on the farm once again."

A few days later, my father was a changed man. He could physically feel the effects of the emotional healing in his body. All the hurt and shame that he had carried around for years had been completely removed. His harsh attitude toward others had been transformed into the meekness of a little child.

My father's encounter with the Lord reminded me of the time when Jesus said, *"Let the little children come to me; do not stop them; for it is to such as these that the kingdom of God belongs. Truly I tell you, whoever does not receive the kingdom of God as a little child will never enter it." And he took them up in his arms, laid his hands on them, and blessed them.*[1]

In the same way, Jesus wants to take all his beloved children into his loving arms. Jesus loves you. He came so that you may have life and have it more abundantly. Don't allow the hurtful events of the past to hinder your ability to live life to the fullest. Allow the Lord's healing power to transform your life today.

7

Accept the Lord's Guidance

One day I met a man named Bill who suffered from chronic depression. Over the years he had visited many psychologists, but his condition continued to grow worse. All that the psychologists wanted to do was to talk about his problems and prescribe various forms of drugs to make him feel better.

When I began working with Bill, I asked him to start the healing meditation with prayer. I wanted him to picture a peaceful nature setting, so I said to him, "Close your eyes and stay focused on the scene until we bring it to completion. I want you to picture yourself in a mountain setting or at the beach."

"I see myself sitting on a rock in the center of a vast meadow," Bill said. "There're butterflies in the air, and I'm surrounded by tall native grass with wildflowers all around me."

"Please ask Jesus to join you," I said. "Picture what he looks like. Ask him to take you back in time to an event that he wants you to work on."

"I see Jesus standing before me, but he's not saying anything," Bill said.

"After you surrender your fears and control over to the Lord, take his hand and follow him wherever he wants you to go."

"Now I see a little boy sitting on the rock," Bill said.

"How does the little boy feel?"

"He doesn't understand life. So many things are uncertain and confusing to him."

"Like what?" I asked.

"Now I see him in front of the school building. The bell just rang and all the other kids have run off to class. He's standing in front of the main entrance, scared to go inside. Mrs. Krobopple is coming to get him. She was inside counting the empty desks, and now she's coming to get him!"

"Don't worry, we are going to have a long talk with Mrs. Krobopple, but first we need some help. I want you and Jesus to enter the scene to help little Billy. Go over and introduce yourself to the little boy. Can you do that? Does he trust you?"

"No! He doesn't trust anybody!"

"Tell him you are here with Jesus to stand up for his rights. Does little Billy trust Jesus?"

"No! Everybody always tries to hurt him."

"What will Mrs. Krobopple do when she catches him outside after the bell has rung?" I asked.

"She will punish him and reprimand him in front of everybody."

"Tell Billy that we will protect him. To prove that we are his friends, we are going to confront Mrs. Krobopple in the hallway before she gets outside. If that's okay with Billy, take his hand and go through the doors. When you see Mrs. Krobopple, tell her how she has been hurting him."

"I see her. She's looking for him, and she's angry. She starts yelling at him."

"I want you to stand up for his rights. Tell the teacher how she is traumatizing this little boy."

"She says, 'This is my school!'"

"Have Jesus tell Mrs. Krobopple whose school this really is. The entire universe belongs to the Lord, including all the precious children whom she has been hurting."

"Jesus told her that her soul was in great danger. I can see that she's sorry because she broke down and started crying," Bill said.

"Ask Mrs. Krobopple to apologize to Billy. After she says that she's sorry, I want you to introduce Jesus to all Billy's friends."

"He doesn't have any friends," Bill said, as tears streamed down his face.

"As soon as everybody sees how little Billy brought Mrs. Krobopple to her knees, he will be the most popular kid in school. Go ahead and tell the kids about Jesus. Have them look down the hall and see Mrs.

Krobopple on her knees before the Lord."

After all the kids cautiously peered out into the hallway, a great celebration broke out in the classroom. Jesus was able to minister to all the schoolchildren, and afterward, Bill was a changed man.

Over the next several days Bill noticed the hindering forces of procrastination and suicidal thoughts that had plagued him for many years had disappeared. He was now able to experience a deeper relationship with the Lord, and accomplish his everyday tasks more effortlessly.

Another man named John also needed to follow the Lord's guidance before he could be set free. Every now and then a paralyzing force of fear would come over him and hinder his ability to make important decisions in life. Before John could be healed, the Lord needed to take him back to a time when he was playing with his brothers and sisters.

There was an old trunk in the basement and the kids were seeing who could fit inside with the lid closed. When it was Johnny's turn, someone shut the latch and locked him inside. No one had the key and all his siblings ran away because no one wanted to get in trouble. After several hours had passed, everybody had forgotten that he was still locked inside the trunk.

To help John heal this negative past experience, we invited the Spirit of Jesus into the healing meditation. The same Jesus that walked through locked doors when the disciples were hiding in the upper room is the same Jesus who wanted to enter the locked trunk to rescue his precious child.

After we invited Jesus into the scene, we asked the Light of the world to illuminate the dark trunk with the brightness of his incredible love. After Jesus was able to minister to little Johnny, we called for his mother to break open the lock. After John forgave his brothers and sisters, he was set free from the paralyzing grip of anxiety that had plagued his life since early childhood.

If you are suffering from some kind of mental, spiritual or physical ailment, ask Jesus to show you the source of the problem. Oftentimes spirits of fear and infirmity have the right to enter our lives through traumatic past experiences. When this happens, most people blame God and think that he is punishing them. Instead of turning to Jesus for healing, many people gradually allow the infirmity to destroy their lives.

If you are suffering from a serious mental, physical or spiritual condition, take some time right now to pray. Go back in time with the Lord, and ask him to show you the source of the problem. Jesus loves you. He took all the sin and sickness of the world upon himself, so that you could be set free. Embrace the Lord's merciful love, and allow yourself to be transformed into the child of God that the Lord intended you to be.

8

Pursue the Lover of Your Soul

All through Sacred Scripture God expresses his enduring love for us. In the Song of Solomon God describes his passion for us in the same way a young man is passionate over his beloved:

How beautiful you are, my love,
how very beautiful!
You have ravished my heart, my sister, my bride,
you have ravished my heart with a
glance of your eyes.[1]

When the young lover from the Song of Solomon travels across town to see his beloved, he knocks on her door and reaches his hand through the lattice, calling out to her, *"Open to me, my sister, my love, my dove, my perfect one."*[2]

The young woman lingers. She says to herself, *"Listen! my beloved is knocking. I had put off my garment; how could I put it on again? I had bathed my feet; how could I soil them?"*[3]

After lingering a while longer and thinking about all the reasons why she does not want to get up, she finally rises to her feet and opens the door. She says, *"I opened to my beloved, but my beloved had turned and was gone."⁴*

After realizing her mistake, the young woman goes out into the night looking for him. *I sought him, but did not find him; I called him, but he gave no answer. Making their rounds in the city the sentinels found me; they beat me, they wounded me, they took away my mantle.⁵*

Without her protective escort, the young woman was vulnerable to attack. She suffered abuse in the town square looking for her beloved. The next day she cried out to her girlfriends, *"I adjure you, O daughters of Jerusalem, if you find my beloved, tell him this: I am faint with love."⁶*

The same is true with our relationship with God. Jesus desperately desires to establish a passionate love affair with all of his beloved children, but when we spend more time with false lovers than we do in true devotion, the Lord may slowly walk away and seem very distant.

When there's nothing better to do, we usually open the door to see if the Lord of the universe is still waiting outside, but oftentimes he has already left. We may go out into the darkness looking for the Light of the world, only to suffer abuse, thinking that God doesn't care.

If you want to establish a passionate love affair with Jesus, you will need to maintain your end of the relationship. Jesus wants your full devotion. It hurts him when you commit the sin of idolatry, praying to false gods, and seeking after false lovers. Jesus wants to be your first and foremost priority in life.

If the Lord seems distant and removed, you may want to start pursuing him. One of the most powerful ways to show him that you are serious was disclosed the day several men asked Jesus a very important question: *"Why do John's disciples and the disciples of the Pharisees fast, but your disciples do not fast?"[7]*

Jesus answered by saying, *"The wedding guests cannot fast while the bridegroom is with them, can they? As long as they have the bridegroom with them, they cannot fast. The days will come when the bridegroom is taken away from them, and then they will fast on that day."[8]*

When the bridegroom walked hand in hand with his beloved bride, it was very easy to approach him and enter into his loving embrace. Now that he has been taken away, it is a little harder to enter the Lord's presence anytime we want, and that is why fasting is so important.

Fasting has the power to break all the ungodly strongholds that may be hindering your ability to commune with the Lord. Fasting opens up a spiritual pipeline from heaven to earth so that you can more easily accept the Lord's healing power. Fasting is the most profound way I know of to experience the divine presence of Christ.

When I first heard about fasting, I was turned off. Someone must have explained the wrong concept to me. Fasting has nothing to do with self-punishment. God takes no pleasure in seeing his beloved children suffer, or even worse, punish themselves in an attempt to gain his approval.

Fasting is converting food hunger into God hunger. When a man fasts, he is denying himself the goodness of physical food in exchange for spiritual food. When we start crying out to God with spiritual hunger, the Lord will feed us supernaturally.

I first started fasting by skipping breakfast one morning. Instantly the fleshly part of my being started making excuses: *It will mess up your diet. You will lose too much weight.* After thinking about what was more important, the pursuit of God or my diet, I decided to give fasting a try.

After I spent most of the morning in prayer, the presence of God was extremely strong. I could feel his loving warmth several times closer than usual. It felt as if the Lord was right beside me the entire time.

Before long, the morning had slipped away, and it was time to break the fast with a bright red apple. I couldn't believe the joy I was experiencing. It was so profound, I decided to go the next day without eating anything.

Before long, I found myself embarking on what my friends call *holy weeks*. I would fast all week on juice and water and ask the Lord to burn all forms of darkness and emotional woundedness out of my soul. I would spend the entire week in prayer, writing healing letters and studying Sacred Scripture.

I usually started the mornings with a glass of mint tea with honey. Around 9 a.m. I would drink a glass of freshly squeezed orange juice. At noon, I would make a protein shake in the blender by adding a frozen banana. In the evening, I would make fresh carrot, tomato and celery juice. I would also take vitamins and eat a little bit of salt every day.

On the third day of the fast, I would be on a spiritual high. The first two days were a little harder. My blood-sugar levels would drop, and I usually got cold and tired, but once I hit the third day, a spiritual pipeline opened up from heaven to earth. My thinking became divinely inspired, and I experienced the divine presence of God like never before.

If you are hungry for a deeper and more intimate relationship with Jesus, you may want to give fasting a try. When you convert all your food hunger into God hunger, Jesus will manifest his Spirit in your life and start feeding you a divine banquet of heavenly cuisine.

What are you waiting for? Embark upon a *holy week* and allow the Lord's miracle-working power to transform your life today.

9

Rest in the Sacred Silence

One day a young man approached his father and asked for his share of the inheritance. The father tried to reason with the boy, but he refused to listen. Every day he grew more demanding, so out of his great love, the father finally granted his request.

A few days later the younger son gathered all he had and traveled to a distant country, and there he squandered his property in dissolute living. When he had spent everything, a severe famine took place throughout that country, and he began to be in need. So he went and hired himself out to one of the citizens of that country, who sent him to his fields to feed the pigs. He would gladly have filled himself with the pods that the pigs were eating; and no one gave him anything.[1]

Every day the young man was separated from his father's house, he grew weaker and more depressed. Soon he became sick. He tried everything to make himself feel better, but nothing he did would comfort the aching need deep within his soul.

One day the young man came to his senses. He

said to himself, *"How many of my father's hired hands have bread enough and to spare, but here I am dying of hunger! I will get up and go to my father, and I will say to him, 'Father, I have sinned against heaven and before you; I am no longer worthy to be called your son; treat me like one of your hired hands.'"*[2]

So he set off and went to his father. But while he was still far off, his father saw him and was filled with compassion; he ran and put his arms around him and kissed him.[3]

The son said to him, *"Father, I have sinned against heaven and before you; I am no longer worthy to be called your son."*[4]

The father said to the slaves, *"Quickly, bring out a robe—the best one—and put it on him; put a ring on his finger and sandals on his feet. And get the fatted calf and kill it, and let us eat and celebrate; for this son of mine was dead and is alive again; he was lost and is found!"*[5]

In the same way, Jesus wants all his beloved children to return to his loving embrace. He wants to feed you with the finest spiritual food, put a gold ring on your finger and clothe you with the garments of royalty.

To embark on this sacred journey, all you need to do is go deep within your heart. There's no need to travel to a distant country looking for love in all the wrong places. The kingdom of heaven resides deep within your soul. All you need to do is enter into the depths of your inner sanctuary.

What are you waiting for? You can start communing with Jesus right now. All you need to do is start listening to his soft-spoken voice. In the same way that sheep listen to the voice of their shepherd, Jesus says, *"My sheep hear my voice. I know them, and they follow me."*[6]

Jesus desperately desires to speak to you. He wants to give you insight into all your daily events. He wants to speak to you with words of wisdom to help you avoid making the wrong decisions in life.

I started listening to the voice of the Good Shepherd many years ago by making a commitment to spend an hour a day practicing contemplative prayer. At first the process was very difficult. I had all kinds of unhealthy thoughts running around inside my head. It took a great amount of discipline to quiet my mind and sit in total silence before the Lord.

After I reached a place of quiet stillness, the Lord's Spirit was able to start ministering to me. When my mind was full of noise and distractions, there was no room for the Lord. As soon as I made room for the soft-spoken voice of Jesus, he appeared to me and started imparting his words of wisdom into my life.

On many occasions, I would just picture Jesus' face and look into his loving eyes. Other times, he would fill me with his loving presence. After spending an hour practicing contemplative prayer in the morning, I felt even more anointed and empowered the rest of the day.

On other occasions the Lord would take me deeper into my heart and start showing me people from my past that I needed to forgive. He wanted to open all the doors of my spiritual house and help me clean out all the trash to make more room for his divine presence.

The Lord wanted to fill my entire spiritual house with his dazzling white light. He wanted to occupy every aspect of my soul, and he was unwilling to share any part of me with darkness, sickness or disease.

In the same way, the Lord wants to take you on a deep, introverted journey. You can start the process right now by eliminating all the noisy distractions from your life. Find a quiet place inside your home and start resting in total silence before the Lord. Invite the Good Shepherd to join you. Learn how to listen to his soft-spoken voice.

Jesus desperately desires to commune with you. Come to him—he is calling you right now. Embrace his love in the quiet stillness of your heart.

10

Enter the Kingdom of Heaven

One day Jesus was sitting by the seashore when a great crowd began to gather. He began teaching the people by saying, *"The kingdom of heaven is like a mustard seed that someone took and sowed in his field; it is the smallest of all the seeds, but when it has grown it is the greatest of shrubs and becomes a tree, so that the birds of the air come and make nests in its branches."[1]*

Again he put before them another parable by saying, *"The kingdom of heaven is like treasure hidden in a field, which someone found and hid; then in his joy he goes and sells all that he has and buys that field."[2]*

After he had finished speaking, his disciples asked, *"Why do you speak to them in parables?"[3]*

He answered, *"To you it has been given to know the secrets of the kingdom of heaven, but to them it has not been given. For to those who have, more will be given, and they will have an abundance; but from those who have nothing, even what they have will be taken away."[4]*

Before you will be able to enter the kingdom of

heaven, you will need to invite the Spirit of Jesus to dwell inside of your heart. Once the Great King makes his home deep within the recesses of your soul, he will become your most valued possession. Like the hidden treasure buried in the field, nothing will compare to his vast richness. He will bestow upon you spiritual wealth that will far surpass anything this world has to offer.

What are you waiting for? Jesus has incredible plans for your life. You have a God who desires to make you his beloved bride. *You shall be a crown of beauty in the hand of the Lord, and a royal diadem in the hand of your God. For as a young man marries a young woman, so shall your builder marry you, and as the bridegroom rejoices over the bride, so shall your God rejoice over you.*[5]

You have been invited to spend the rest of eternity with God in heaven. What are you waiting for? *Do you not know that in a race the runners all compete, but only one receives the prize? Run in such a way that you may win it.*[6] Throw aside every weight and hindrance that clings so close and start running the race in such a way as to win the everlasting prize.

The time is now—the kingdom of heaven is at hand!

The Healing Letter Exercise

1. Spend some time practicing contemplative prayer and ask the Lord to show you the situation he wants you to work on.

2. After you identify a hurtful past event that needs healing, try to separate the situation from everything else that has happened to you. Instead of trying to work through years of emotional abuse in one letter, try to isolate the experience and keep working on the situation until it is resolved.

3. Begin the exercise from a prayerful and meditative state of mind. Find a quiet place where you can be alone with the Lord. Make sure you have plenty of tissues and the necessary writing supplies.

4. Picture the person who hurt you in your imagination. Imagine that person can hear everything you are about to say. If the person is deceased, picture them in heaven standing next to Jesus.

5. Begin writing your letter with the words, *I'm angry because you hurt me!* Tell this person all the ways that he or she has hurt you by his or her careless and disrespectful actions. Keep writing the words *I'm angry*, over and over again. Vent all your anger on paper. Don't worry about spelling or grammar; just release everything that needs to be said.

6. After you vent all your anger, move on to any fears that you may have experienced. How has this person affected your life? Describe how the consequences of his or her careless actions have carried forward into your present-day relationships.

7. After you vent any fears or guilty feelings, get in touch with your sadness. Tell this person what you wanted to happen that didn't. If you're writing to your father say, *I'm sad because I wanted a better relationship with you. I wanted you to treat me like a beloved son or daughter. I wanted your love and support.*

8. Conclude your letter with anything else you need to say to this person, and then begin a new letter by picturing the person who hurt you in a completely healed state. Picture them in heaven standing next to Jesus. Imagine this person full of God's love, and because they are full of God's love, allow them to offer you an apology.

9. Start your apology letter by saying, *I'm sorry for hurting you. You didn't deserve to be treated like that. I'm so sorry. Please forgive me.* Write down all the loving words that you need to hear.

10. Conclude your apology letter with prayer. Release the person who hurt you into the Lord's hands. Ask Jesus to wash away any negativity that you may have picked up by accepting this person's abuse. Surrender this person to the Lord, and if appropriate, ask Jesus to break all unhealthy soul-ties.

11. Allow Jesus to speak to you through a closure letter. Accept the Lord's love and forgiveness. Allow the Lord's love and forgiveness to flow into your heart and cleanse you of all curses, resentment and negativity.

12. Ask the Lord to show you if there's anything else that you need to release. Allow yourself to fall into the Lord's arms and be permanently set free—free to be the child of God the Lord intended you to be.

Notes

Introduction
1. John 4:9.
2. John 4:10.
3. John 4:11.
4. John 4:13–14.
5. John 4:15.
6. John 4:16.
7. John 4:17.
8. John 4:17–18.
9. John 4:18.
10. John 4:28–29.
11. John 10:10.
12. John 7:37–38.

1 — Offer an Invitation to Jesus
1. John 14:23.
2. 1 John 5:10 & 12.

2 — Acknowledge the Painful Truth
1. Matthew 26:31.
2. Matthew 26:33.
3. Matthew 26:34.
4. Matthew 26:35.
5. Luke 22:56.
6. Luke 22:57.
7. Luke 22:58.
8. Luke 22:59.
9. Luke 22:60.
10. Luke 22:61.
11. Luke 22:62.
12. John 21:3.
13. John 21:3.
14. John 21:6.
15. John 21:7.
16. John 21:10.
17. John 21:15.
18. John 21:15.
19. John 21:16.
20. John 21:16.
21. John 21:17.
22. John 21:17.
23. John 21:17.

3 — Wash in His Life-Giving Water
1. John 13:5.
2. John 13:6.
3. John 13:7.
4. John 13:8.
5. John 13:8.
6. Psalm 103:11–12.

6 — Fall into His Loving Arms
1. Mark 10:14–16.

8 — Pursue the Lover of Your Soul
1. Song of Solomon 4:1 & 9.
2. Song of Solomon 5:2.
3. Song of Solomon 5:2 & 3.
4. Song of Solomon 5:6.
5. Song of Solomon 5:6–7.
6. Song of Solomon 5:8.
7. Mark 2:18.
8. Mark 2:19–20.

9 — Rest in the Sacred Silence

1. Luke 15:13–16.
2. Luke 15:17–19.
3. Luke 15:20.
4. Luke 15:21.
5. Luke 15:22–24.
6. John 10:27.

10 — Enter the Kingdom of Heaven

1. Matthew 13:31–32.
2. Matthew 13:44.

3. Matthew 13:10.
4. Matthew 13:11–12.
5. Isaiah 62:3 & 5.
6. 1 Corinthians 9:24.

Back Cover Text —
Matthew 11:28.

About the Author

Robert Abel's purpose and passion in life is speaking God's truth unto today's generation. He lives in Denver, Colorado, where he helps others heal through counseling sessions and healing seminars.

If you would like Robert to speak at your parish, or if you would like to share your healing testimony, please contact: **www.HealingPowerMinistries.com**

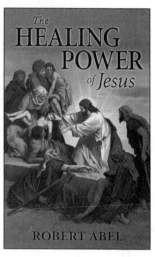

If you would like to participate in our healing ministry, please consider spreading the message of *Healing Power for the Heart* to everybody you know who needs to experience more of God's love. To purchase additional copies of this book for ministry purposes, or to make a donation, please use the following information:

Number of Copies	Ministry Price
6	$29
12	$49
18	$69

These prices include tax and free shipping within the United States. For shipments to other countries, please contact us. Thank you for your generous support.

Mail your payment to:

Valentine Publishing House
Healing Power for the Heart
P.O. Box 27422
Denver, Colorado 80227